homespun mysticism

by dj hill

ISBN: 978-1-7327909-4-0

Library of Congress Control Number: 2018911578

DJ Hill

www.djhill-writer.com

Published in the USA
Printed in Colorado

Light of the Moon, Inc. - Publishing Division
Book Design/Production/Consulting
Carbondale, Colorado
www.lightofthemooninc.com

Homespun Mercies

ACKNOWLEDGMENTS

I would like to thank the editors of the following magazines, anthologies,
newspapers, and journals in which these poems and collages
first appeared, sometimes in different forms:

Daily Sentinel: "One Crimson Leaf." *The Fulcrum:* "Bonferroni Stew" and "Slip."
Red Bird Chapbooks Weekly Read: "Drive By Shoes." *Red Flag Poetry:* "Ars Poetica."
The Rumpus: "Late at Night," "Rockabye Baby," and "What Did I Know of Love."
Young Ravens Literary Review: "An Apology to My Inner Poet."

~ ~ ~

Many thanks to everyone who contributed to this project over the past two decades
and those who were instrumental in this book coming into being: editor Jenniey Tallman,
my son Tom who edited the earliest drafts, photographer Shawn Tolle at Sopris Printing,
Alyssa Ohnmacht and Olivia Savard at Light of the Moon, Inc. - Publishing Division,
Gran Farnum Printing and Publishing, webmaster Christine Rousu at So It Goes Design,
publicist Corey Johnson at Scintilla Media, professors and authors Cullen Bailey Burns,
John Colburn, Patricia Francisco, Deborah Keenan, Beth Mayer, Anna George Meek,
Juliet Patterson, Mary Rockcastle, Katrina Vandenberg, artist Holly Roberts,
studio mates at Anderson Ranch Arts Center and Making Art Safely in Santa Fe,
Don Messec, Chris Meyer, Melissa Borman, Nancy Eike at Tiger Oak Publications,
Jill Greenhalgh at the Century College Foundation, Sheryl Rosenbloom and Ganesh,
The Creative Writing Programs at Century College and Hamline University,
fellow students and the Poet Squad, The Redstone Inn,
Sarah Roy and Red Brick Center for the Arts, The Launchpad,
Carbondale Arts, the creator who made it all possible,
and friends and family who encouraged me along the way. Thank you.

And to Kathleen Jesme, I finally found the way in.

I dedicate this book to Bob,
with love and gratitude~

CONTENTS

COLLAGES

*We shall not cease from exploration, and the end of all our exploring
will be to arrive where we started and know the place for the first time.*

T. S. Eliot

Ars Poetica

Untie the dead weight of expectations, fears, facades, and let them slowly drip from your burdened shoulders, a descending pool around weary ankles.

Peel the doubt and dread, releasing one arm at a time, until your head is the last to be set free, the moment you panic you just can't breathe.

Shimmy out of your imperfections, baggy or skinny, those parts you've contained or hidden, hoping to sidestep judgment.

Slip out of the undergarments that cradle those intimate, vulnerable crevasses, not allowing yourself reprieve until the last silky or cotton shred is discarded.

Glance down and marvel at that glorious heap on the dull, wooden floor.

Only then will I listen to your fears: You haven't accomplished enough, remain afraid of the future, the dark, getting older, of being alone.

Expose your innermost self and let your heart beat wildly

tender heart

Untitled

I

Tonight I would love God
with skin on

To behold his face of benevolence
or shadows of consternation

Kindly wisdom
or parental disapproval

I deserve them all

II

When we sleep together
I transgress the mortal space
of our coupling, spoons
twisting, wrapped in waning
skin. I dream I wander
through memories
of youth, taut and tenacious
fertile landscapes untilled
overturned earth lush
with possibilities

III

How often I searched for God
in churches, temples, pilgrimages
vestiges of holy prayer

But found him in prairies pregnant
with fragrant blossoms I could not name
clandestine forests, the scent of loam

Galaxies brimming with celestial
fireballs, luminous lanterns of light
beckoning me heavenward

IV

And as our positions shift
the rows in my subconscious
grow increasingly ragged, windrows
of spent stalks turned brittle

Sunlight dipping deeper into
finite horizons, I pull you closer
our collective body heat
protection from impending winter

What Was I to Know of Love

The first time a boy told me he loved me, I was in 6th grade
Mr. Evenocheck's class, kept in from recess for failing
to complete the required assignment—constructing my spider
body from wire and yarn so it could hang with the others

As my classmate and I sat in silence, winding the bodies
in wool to hide the crudeness of our forms
and playground screams wafted through open windows
he passed a crumbled note, *I love you* scrawled in pencil

The second time a boy said he loved me I learned love
is skin deep: his Hawaiian mocha, mine milky transparency
I didn't know the lines of love were so clear cut
sometimes it's best love remain unspoken

The next time a boy said he loved me, I learned love
can split a body open, spilling its sacrificed secrets
returning the contents to the vessel damaged
hairline cracks invisible to the naked eye

The next boy waited

The next time a boy said, *I think I'm in love*
five words a welcome refrain, restrained
plenty of time to unwrap the body
bend the wire looser, or tighter

The next time, there was no such thing
as love—the mildewed dorm room, curtains pulled
Carrie in flames and the spider's web sticky
I think I'm in love became refuge

The last time a boy said the word
the edges were raw, the wire exposed
soft wool covering rusted metal
the ruined web swept aside

heart

thump thump, thump thump
one heart alone makes up a single rhythm
it is true I beat but not for you,
nor love, nor passion
not for fright or fear or folly

i beat as that is what life requires
not a perfectly formed specimen
the companion of Cupid's arrow

purple, pulsing, palpitations
pushing lifeblood through paper-thin tendrils
all day, every day, without end

until I stop, in which case you stop
and all is quiet, as we lay down
our arrows at love's feet

SECRETS

Big brown box dropped down   cooling the desert
Immovable fortress move   moved   moving closer
To luminescence   Scorpions scatter   sacrificial
Sacrament safe on sand   Impenetrable   my heart
Like scorpions   lethal   shelled body armor
Keeping words out   I'm safe   This big brown box
Blocking light   surrounding softness of heart   scorpions
Dodge arrows sharpened   shadows snake closer in sand
Shadows holding secrets   I hold secrets
Alone   the box   out of place   out of harried
Mind   the scorpion I cannot see   it follows
Beware what waits outside these walls   sacraments
We take taste bitter   the sting I didn't see coming

Spec Lake

Oh, the summer when time was bottled

Fishing poles packed in the back
of paneled station wagons, all for the sake
of sunburns and sunfish, water and watermelon
sand between toes and sun bursts in eyes, fireflies
and campfires, burning embers, and the day I first met you

Oh, those days filled with baseball
long bronzed legs and sun kissed hair in sweltering heat

You waiting in the outfield
stirring desire I couldn't explain

Switching off the headlights, moonlight
danced on your broad shoulders, tan-lined waist, shadows
innocent by the lake where you ran down the grassy slope
headlong, and I

hesitated, not knowing what it meant to be
free, following you, breathless, into inky black water

Matrimonial Villanelle

Wedding china, lead glass crystal
Drawers and drawers of English silver
Lie in the midst of your affection
The knives silent, the spoons quiver

Tines and edges, newly polished
Pitch black spots yet undetected
The table we kept so perfectly set

Day by day, facades do tarnish
Minds and hearts, loyalties questioned
The knives silent, the spoons quiver

Losing one piece and then another
Remnants at once so new
But what's there to do without the other

His face looks heavenward, mine a mask
Downward cast
The knives silent, the spoons quiver

We said we'd stay together
But forever
Drawers and drawers of English silver
The knives silent, the spoons shiver

Tell Me Again

"You'll get used to it."
        But I told you
        I want the same color on the ceiling as the walls,
I said to the painter, temporarily blinded
by ceiling white, the hue we chose
by default.

        Who doesn't choose ceiling white for a ceiling?

I murmured to my rebellious self
the one who feigned delight
at gold jewelry instead of white
Chocolate cake when, God forbid
I wanted angel.

And yes to reruns of chick flicks
        once is simply not enough.

So no I don't want my ceiling
to be ceiling white, even if my fellow
residents of planet Earth
insist on the exact same color.

How many times you surprised me
with a forest green turtleneck,
socks, sweater, Schwinn,
running attire
        but I never liked forest green.

Maybe because it was your favorite
and never mine
        that honor reserved
        for buttery yellow
the color you never gave me.

Last Night I Dreamt You Left Me

You were growing weary
of the way I was
                    or wasn't

You didn't look back
You didn't mourn

How soon I became
an afterthought

I awoke, heartbroken
a familiar body
rolled into mine
and somehow I knew I was already

                                        gone.

Haikus and After

Part 1

The hawk circles field
As mouse scampers under brush
Spared until next time

A brown December
Children lick frosted windows
Dreaming of snowmen

Eyes of bending birch
Glimpse their frozen reflection
Fish trapped until spring

The arrogance of
Belonging he held tightly
Until solitude

The pawns hesitate
Under the queen's watchful gaze
Their fate all but sealed

Menthol shaving cream
The scent of pipe tobacco
Father's tangled brow

Handprints on windows
Tiny feet on wooden stairs
Children grown too soon

He left this morning
She smokes candy cigarettes
Staring into rain

Sun peeks through trees, bare
Stripped naked by winter winds
Earth cloaked in silence

Part 2

They sit in silence
In the house with wooden stairs
As sun peaks through trees, bare
Chess pieces standing idle

The scent of pipe tobacco
Her watchful gaze
Who were they when

The children were young
The mouse was spared
Before earth lay dormant

His arrogance he held tightly
The hawk circling fields

She smokes candy cigarettes
Staring through frosted windows
Fish trapped until spring

familias bodies

Late at Night My Mind Goes Walking

                              Wandering streets, the towns, places I called

Home but the fires of the past have been snuffed

                              Out, my mind locked, no skeleton key can open

My father used to keep a collection

                              Keys tied up with twine, keys to someone

Else's car, their home, a life

                              My aunt once told me she dreamed her house

Had a secret room, one which held everything

                              She loved most. I used to have that dream

But now when my mind finds the right key

                              The house is vacant, filled with empty

Boxes   FRAGILE   matchbooks

                              A weary mind, searching for its own past

Returns to bed, my body warm, strikes a match

                              Turned flame, the house a slow burn

Lost and
Found
in the
Wood

Independence Pass

Slow, steady rain cloaked the mountain
Obscuring my vision

Windshield wipers, hard pressed
To keep the inevitable at bay

Laying the course
With no purpose other than

This moment and I thought
Who would know if this aging

Piece of metal and parts
Plummeted headstrong

Into the cavernous ravine
Its craggy fingers releasing

Bits of flesh and sinew scattered
A freefall into hallowed air

HEADLINES

I read about it in the paper, on the subway on my
way to work, how Mick Jagger's girlfriend had
taken her own life, something about a scarf and the
handle of a French door which should have made
me feel a tinge of sadness, wondering how Mick
would survive the loss of his significant other or
deal with the shock, the publicity, the legal battles
sure to come now that his dead girlfriend's fortune
proved to be nothing on paper, but instead I wanted
to know about the scarf and the French door, about
whether someone actually plans that or does she
spot a favorite scarf hanging or folded neatly in her
walk-in closet and say, "By god, that piece of
Versace silk will do the job," what with the thinking
and tying, the tying and thinking, the juxtaposition
of fashion accessory with lethal accomplice, was
there a moment where she contemplated her
options, like I did while reading the paper, on the
subway, on my way to work, loosening my scarf.

Sidney, Montana

The Homestead Act of 1862 tempted with free land and the good life. Cultivate and work it for five years, it is yours. But as they say, nothing is free. My grandfather's uncalloused hands moved effortlessly over piano keys, yet failed to grasp the yoke of hardship that free land requires. Grasshoppers feasting on acres of tender shoots, soybeans or corn, second-hand machinery destined to break, down the road to free land, with empty cupboards and treeless landscapes, one room hovels with dirt floors and rats and rainless culverts, occasionally flooding to swallow up a child. "You'll most certainly go to hell," my grandmother cried, as my grandfather diligently worked the Sabbath field, watching the fine, silvery powders of the good life slowly sift away.

Annie Oakley

after E. E. Cummings

Annie Oakley
legend
         who they say was birthed
         in that Willowdell log cabin, taught to sew and decorate
         and in the spring loaned out
         damn near a slave
         to an unnamed family with needy infant
         false promises of greenbacks and education
         by the wolves of Preble County
         but she wouldn't have it, Watanya Cicilla
         she fled to hunt and trap and shoot and by god
         how her rifle freed her mama from the burden of debt
Near famous was she in
         Buffalo Bill's Wild West Show
         Butler with his bet underestimated
Miss Annie Oakley
         Twenty five shots it took him
         to lose yet win her favor
         Little Miss Sure Shot
                  Raising her .22 caliber Smith and Wesson
         To split-a-playing-card-faster-than-you-can-say   fire

Chief Sitting Bull
                   and I want to know
Did you think to watch your back
Buffalo Bill

Slip

Today began with that morning blur
the one we swear being prepared will erase

Mismatched socks, misplaced keys
the slip that, *oh god*
somehow replaced the dress
absentmindedly forgotten

As you step out of your car—
full of water bottles, wrappers,
school papers, debris
of a life well-lived, evidence

you store there until that transcendent day
when stars and moons align
and your family is perfect, your husband
centered and all is organized
in rubber-sealed containers

which leaves you alone
the source of all ills
you in the parking lot
you in the slip
minus the dress.

Ties That Bind

Women need friends
        as flowers need rain-
                We are destined to droop
                        without friendships' refreshment
Women need friends
        as flowers need rain-
                We would shrivel, wilt, and die
                        without someone to share our grief
Women need friends
        as flowers need rain-
                We unfurl at the sunrise of new love
                        knowing dawn awaits should love end
Women need friends
        as flowers need rain-
                We have each other as witnesses as our petals close
                        that we, indeed, did bloom

Lucretia *after Rembrandt*

They have said the depth of my despair
Reverberates down these hallowed halls
Stuccoed walls bearing the weight of betrayal

Rapes pungent smell leaves this aging frame
A spreading stain permeates the landscapes
Of virginal pastorals created by mortal men

As I watch the girl with her saffron curls
Pause, transfixed by a bloodied blade
Unaware, I'm afraid, of impending rain.

earth songs

Fall Sneaks In

This morning, as darkening clouds
edged out the bright sky
I realized how I feel about the fall
my favorite season
the welcomed interloper

           separating seasons of the same Mother

Summer, with its lackadaisical attitude
and bronzed swagger
And winter with its holier than thou
love me or leave me challenge

           yet fall sneaks in

When our minds are preoccupied
with backpacks and back to school
First days and final goodbyes
distractions that make us forget

           another year or years have passed

As leaves begin their annual change
transforming barren landscapes into majestic tapestries
While our spirits rise and soar until
warm winds shift, casting leaves adrift

           the tough broad in white taking their place

Today

Today I'm going to pretend
I owe the world nothing

No good morning salutation
No offer of tea, espresso, coffee
soothed by cream
No good will, no awe, no wonder

No reminder or apology
for something I've said, or forgotten
No text, email, or phone call back
letter, fax, or response

No thank you notes written
with adoring sentiments
or checks handed over grudgingly
for rooms left unclean, driveways
yet unsealed

Instead, today you are on your own world

I will stop for a late morning latte,
maybe a scone. Perhaps countless hours
perusing bookstores for exotic travel books
I will never buy

You will have to pull out
your own seat, open your own
door, fill up your own schedule
find your own sunshine

Planting Tulips

New life will come haltingly with the spring
Tender buds, growing to shoots, pushing forth
to take a breath of life affirming air. You and I
having plunged the fleshy teardrops into unforgiving ground
wait in hopefulness for the cycle of life yet to come
Come springtime, sweet springtime, when the Earth
renews my partner in life, in love, and I
anticipating the spreading smile its bouquet will bring
As the blossoms unfurl
becoming more lovely with each pastel petal
We will remember that gray, October day
when our fingers ached and bones were chilled.

One Crimson Leaf

lay bare
against the grayness
of fall

One lured my eye
to this last show
of fiery red
its yellowed veins

and
halted my steps
to finger-jagged edges
symmetrical design

One crimson leaf
in a world gone numb
made my heart
jump

Congress Avenue

Winged creatures rendered dormant
by things yet unseen, inexplicable
darkness, even to them

Under the Ann Richards Memorial
Bridge, crowds line the overpass
park in kayaks and riverboats

At dusk on All Hallows Eve
we watch, wait for the great rapture
of countless souls held captive

A growing flutter from deep
within, as silhouettes dart
across murky skies, the dread

of the unknown we fear, Congress
Avenue bats plunging deeper
into obscurity, their gossamery
released to devour the night air

Final Flight

Her tiny frame dropped from the sky
On cold gray concrete fell
As autumn showed its shifting face
I stooped to bid farewell.

A single wing raised in defeat
Her end had come mid-flight
Eyes fixed on something seen ahead
Green belly still shown bright.

Fragile wings and weary heart
They too would now find rest
I gathered up those harvest leaves
To shape a burial nest.

And there I laid her tenderly
In a field under clear blue skies
Where was my weathered friend headed
Last chance she had to fly.

Realism and American Literature of the 1860s

The first word of the assignment
stared back from the page

a lone reed

And I thought what else
is there to write that hasn't
been said by historians

or rambling lit professors
for after all, who would care
But the heron swooped

over the waterfall turned koi
pond, so I watched a bit
to gauge his intention

his form remaining motionless
As the koi tail seductively
waved

its scales glistening
And every so often
the heron would raise

a leg as though to change
his mind, never
fully committing to the task

Sleeping Tree

Oh what a fool
                          a fool I'd be in March
the month deceptions
                          rise to believe
the sleeping robin-
                          filled tree who's mocking
call my hope compromised
                          the branches brim
with chestnut breasts
                          as yellow beaks
yet unrestrained sing melodic trills
                          with expectant hearts
a chorus of music only spring
                          can claim but snow
and chill my mind do cloud
                          as feathered flock
suddenly takes flight and leaves
                          only grayness where sun
had given promise of light
                          And now I await
their triumphant return, robins
                          to alight the sleeping tree
robins bringing spring, singing
                          spring to me.

Jack fell down and broke his crown, and Jill came tum-bling af-ter.

Jack and Jill went up the hill to fetch a pail of wa - ter.

Favorite Nursery Songs

Rock-a-bye, baby, thy cradle is green;

Father's a nobleman, mother's a queen;

And Betty's a lady, and wears a gold ring;

And Johnny's a drummer, and drums for the King.

The little dog laughed to see such sport,

And the dish ran away with the spoon.

Humpty Dumpty sat on a wall,

Rock-a-bye, baby, on the tree top,

When the wind blows, the cradle will

Hey, diddle, diddle! The cat

The cow jumped over the moon.

Rock-a-bye, Baby

Ma - ry had a lit - tle lamb, its fleece was white as snow.

Mother Goosed Sonnet

If you are early
        your mother once said
her voice a whir dancing
        inside your head
above the clouds you lick the sky
        and thread the eye
of a lullaby, while little boy blue
        done blown his horn, the sheep
in the barnyard the cows eating corn
        while you row and you row
till you sow what you reap
        by then you have little
if nothing to eat. But hey did
        the middle still fiddle
with rings while Humpty
        still grumpy, collects all his things
Mary, quite merry, contrarily
        calls Jack and Jill
up the hill till one of them falls
        in the bucket with luck
you eventually find
        the bird with the worm
yes, all in due time.

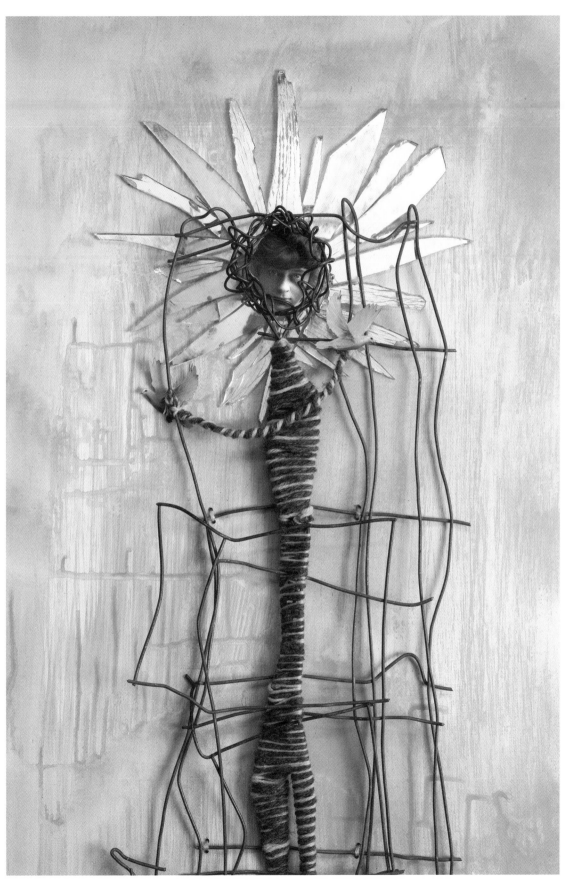

invocations

An Apology to My Inner Poet

Who took the day off
after a brief stint in subzero temps.
He didn't even call in sick.

I hear he took a red-eye,
wooed to warmer climates—
bronzing oil, Ray-Bans, spandex Speedo
two sizes too small.

Perhaps a Greyhound with his duffel bag
in tow, regaling my reluctant nature
to his fellow travelers: *This poet?*
Total slacker.

I can't say I blame him.

Every day he perches
in the corner of the study, tapping
his fingers on the armrest,
his gaze piercing the back of my head

while I clean what is already spotless,
invent to-do lists, sharpen
already pointed pencils
shift a word from here to there

Alone in this pristine castle
hoping tomorrow he will call
I'll ask to meet for drinks, promise to
change
knowing he will take me back.

Fort Snelling

Rows of dead slumber
under eclipsing skies
Maples changing guard
before nature lays down
a white blanket of silence

Blades of trodden grass
tombs and immortal time
muffle the world
the land of the living

Until eventide
when souls grow
restless, turning
pages of life unlived

And ever so softly
the murmurs come
low as a whisper,
the chant of the dead

"And it came to pass
in an eventide
that David arose
from his bed, and walked
upon the roof of the kings' palace"

So too these souls rise, transfixed
freed of limitations, epitaxial
wafers, semiconductors
pulsing their cosmic lifeblood

Phantom pains misplaced
limbs replaced
in a moment of inspired
immortality

I Met God in a Sushi Bar

On a weekday before Thanksgiving
As bleary-eyed travelers shuffled
Through concourses brimming
With the thankful, and God we are

Thankful, he appeared weary
Shoulders slumped, eyes
Transfixed by banks of flat screens
Proliferating global violence

Over steaming edamame sprinkled
With whirling sirens signaling
Horror, God paused to give
Thanks, amidst body bags of endless

Blasphemy, travelers avoiding his gaze
Children purging God
From the annual feast, children blessed
By default, by chance spared

From events across the sea
A Mali hotel under siege

Drive By Shoes

Driving along the freeway today
listening to MPR's debate
on the threat of ISIS, terrorists enlisting
even from this state of Minnesota nice

when a Dodge Caravan speeding past
rolled down its window
and out soared a single shoe.
No explanation or apology,

no brake lights signaling
a change of heart,
just an errant loafer discarded
for not carrying its weight.

So this is how it happens, I thought
recalling the sight of another lone shoe
kicked to the median strip
of our shoe lined interstates,

while its counterpart
of sole and heel
trembles on the floorboard,
a last ditch effort to escape detection.

Adjustments

tell him of the rupture

        S-5

                skilled surgeon darning
                frayed edges

        raw
        seeping

                a checklist of causes. car
                accident? sports injury?

childhood trauma?

                pointing to the x-rays

        vertebrae
        condensed
        bone-on-bone
        fusing

                vertigo, migraines, imbalance

aftermath

                he says decay takes time

        receptors
        short circuit
        the machine
        of body

needing overhaul

                a root cause for new ills

        Occiput
        C-1
        Disjointed

                as he cradles my head,
                a sharp twist

        crack
        crack
        crack

a hieroglyphic history
of hurt and healing.

God as a Patriarchal God

That guy I've known since Sunday school
Our Father, who art in heaven
Long before gendering God was an option
When we all swallowed the same host

Father, Son and Holy Ghost
Some desire Mary as ceremonial head
But tables set in the days of Rome
Kept Hail Mary reserved for sin

Lead us not into temptation
Of haggling over specifics
Assuming God "of all that was
And ever will be" is confined
To one gender, one color, one image

For thine is the kingdom and the power and the glory.
Can I get an Amen? May all God's children say, "Amen!"

Mother Earth

I am the rain pinging off shingles,
the windows of the place you call
home on a Monday, as you dream
of snowfall, the bluster of winter

I wash the grit
from your porch, your driveway, the statue
of Mary, eyes lifted to the sky
It is all made clean

I water your lawn, green
in December, the month of snowmen
Spring ushered in silently, months
before her time

I fall on the ice as it turns soft,
then vanishes back into itself
as fish rise to the surface, warmed
by the change in biological

clocks and cars stand idle
on entrance ramps, waiting
for their chance to merge
into the humming pace of progress

Bonferroni Stew

I drift into a fitful sleep, as my troubled mind stirs
Ingredients added one by one, pot
Worn by wear, metal and copper, scorched
By too many uses over time, spoonfuls
Of alphas and beta in my statistical soup, blended over flame
And even in my dreams I see the square roots simmer

One by one, into the mix the samples go, bubbles
Form round the central tendency, nominal variables stirring
My mind from sleep, disturbed by blue flame,
Turned orange. Mean, mode, median, added to the stockpot
Sums of squared errors, peppered and measured, stirred
With rank order repetition lest it burn

While I ponder my power tables, flames
Climb higher, as I add cups of raw scores, simmering
Just enough for Bonferroni to demand a spoonful
"Not enough!" As he adds a splash of Cramer's phi, ladling
Degrees of freedom into the plentiful pan
Confidence intervals spilling down the sides, singed

My hand, hot as I wipe partial correlation coefficients, burned
The small entering my senses even in sleep, blazing fire
Dichotomizing the phoenix from the ashes
Numerators and denominators in the double boiler
I toss and turn, knowing the correlation between cook
And confidence limits is a delicate balance, I churn

The thick robustness, sampling just enough dollops
To keep it all straight, keep it holding constant, teaspoons
Are more than I can measure, errors, errors, errors burn
My confidence interval, but I focus on the task, stir
The difference scores, tend the grand means, fry
Up main effect, but stay focused on the simmering

Sampling, sums of all the parts, stewing in the pot
On my stove, in my dreams, in my stockpot
Of standard deviations from myself, cooked
Overcooked, pureed probabilities, reduced by fire
Once independent, now congealed by flame
Theorems burned into a restless mind, stirred

When exhaustion whips my values I step away from the pot
Watching the pan burn, the crusted spoon
The ingredients bubble, simmer, stew.

Harry

My friend called to say
she's driving her mother
with her dog Harry
to the animal hospital

She didn't say what ails the canine
sharing instead her mother's choosing
to pass the time on her cell
making chit chat
with her boyfriend

as poor, miserable Harry
lay languishing on the stiff back seat
hardly raising his head
or mournful eyes
until her mother said to the boyfriend

Couldn't you just talk to Harry?
Hearing your voice might make him feel better.

So the mother, not the friend
cradled the phone close
to the pooch's long, chocolate ear
and the two listened
as boyfriend crooned

It's ok boy. You'll be ok.
Good dog. Good boy.

Harry didn't lift his sorrowful
head from the red vinyl seat
His eyes seemed to say to mother, boyfriend, friend-
Good god, it's all come to this.

24 Hours

the sun still slumbers
at this hour, shuffling
'cross hardwood floors
nightlight illuminating
familiar terrain, scarlet
teapot blowing off steam
me, knowing copious
cups of caffeinated inspiration
can't transform weekdays
mourning the loss of weekend
freedom lost pulling on armor
heading back to battle

nightfall, driving, gazing up
at countless stars, dimly
lit hours before it starts
again wondering is this all there is, god
is there purpose to all this
madness, I think I see, god
glancing back from his celestial window

In August of 2017, DJ Hill took a one week workshop with me at Anderson Ranch in Snowmass, Colorado. The workshop was about mixing media, but what it was really about was listening to and connecting with one's inner voice. DJ was, to put it simply, quite amazing in her ability to put together her images, learning the processes quickly and accessing her intuitive, creative self. By the end of the week she had put together an astounding body of work, and even more astounding because, as I later learned, she had had almost no experience in the visual arts. Almost a year later, DJ took another workshop with me in Santa Fe. The focus was to create a cover for her upcoming book of poetry, Homespun Mercies. *I watched in astonishment as she produced an image that went way beyond her skill set, seeming to follow an almost magical trail of breadcrumbs that led her, on the last day of class, to produce "Release," a seemingly simple but, in reality, a complicated image that spoke directly to the poems that would live beneath the cover.*

~ Holly Roberts, artist

NOTES ON THE COVER ART, *Release*

I saw the
angel in the
marble and
carved until I
set him free.

Michelangelo

May 28, 2018. It had been a difficult few months. While on a walk to clear my head, I stumbled upon a vertical piece of fencing. Something made me pick it up and bring it home. As I placed the rusted wire in my kitchen window, the morning sunshine illuminated the silhouette of a woman's body. The fencing stayed in the window until I traveled to Santa Fe in May of 2018 for a workshop with mixed media artist Holly Roberts. Having recently committed to publishing my first collection of poetry, my editor insisted I create the cover and Holly's workshop seemed the perfect place to do it.

The night before leaving, I tossed and turned debating what images and supplies to bring. I thought of the fencing which led to me to think about the 'woman' in the fencing, and how to turn an ugly piece of discarded metal into a compelling image. And like any gift of serendipity, I suddenly recalled the antique button box my parents had given me. Tiptoeing out of bed, I found the box in the basement filled with hundred-year-old yarn, buttons, and silk thread. Something told me this also needed to make the trek to New Mexico.

The workshop was held at the home of Don Messec, a skilled photographer and creator of the "Making Art Safely" workshops located just outside the city limits. Don constructed the classroom space in the desert complete with a vintage trailer acting as the only restroom facility—eliminating the temptation of technology.

Day 1. As with Holly's previous classes, the first task was to prepare our work tables, gesso and sand our boards, then experiment with paint and textures which acted as backdrops for what was to follow. I am NOT a painter. The skill of what I considered the 'true artists' in the room was intimidating. None of that, however, seemed to matter once we got started. Each artist dove into their work, only coming up for air during Holly's demonstrations or lunchtime, whichever came first. By the end of the first day I had a collection of boards in different sizes and colors. As I returned to the rental later that evening, the rosy hue of the Santa Fe foothills seemed confirmation for why I had come.

Day 2. At nine in the morning, I had the painted backdrops, the fencing, and a box of old photographs and memorabilia, but no clue what should come next. Holly continued her demonstrations of photographic processes and, seeing my apprehension, sat down to help clarify my vision. She spoke of aesthetic choices—how everything from paint color to the position of the hands could enhance or detract from the piece. But first the subject had to be brought into being. So I gathered up the fencing and yarn, settled into a solitary lawn chair in the soothing Santa Fe sun, and proceeded to wind and unwind the coarse century old yarn (juxtaposed with new yarn) until the form appeared. Something about the old and the new, and the cool metal wrapped in the safety of wool spoke to me, and I left that day satisfied that "she" had been born.

Day 3. Problem solving. Storytelling. Technical skills. These became the buzz words for the day. Now that "she" had revealed herself, what was the next step? How could I attach a piece of warped metal to the prepared board? Which board/color choice? And was the goal to have a finished piece or to only create to satisfy a photographer's lens? Once the decision was made to bring her fully into existence, I became an apprentice to those whose skills surpassed my own. Artist Chris Meyer, who was assisting with the class, demonstrated how to drill holes with a manual drill, fashion a sewing needle from a piece of metal, and adhere glass to a painted surface—insisting I try them myself.

Day 4. I awoke overcome with anxiety. While great headway had been made the previous day, something was missing. I couldn't put my finger on what it was or how I would overcome this challenge. The night before, my husband and I had toured the St. Francis Cathedral in downtown Santa Fe. A statue had recently been unveiled reminiscent of the Lady of Guadalupe. With her sunburst halo and knowing gaze, Mary Untier of Knots, hit me at a soul level.

Driving to the workshop that morning, a glint of light off to the side of the road caught my attention. How many times had I felt a prompting to stop and investigate but instead drove on? Not this morning. I did a U-turn and scanned the field to see what had drawn me back. There, past the barbed wire, lay a large, plate glass mirror shattered. Helped by a walking stick found earlier in the week and (fortunately) no rattle-snakes, I fished out a container full of shards and headed to the studio.

There is a wonderous excitement when what you have dreamed or imagined comes to pass. I carried the pieces into my workspace and began to fashion a halo. Some shards were too large or oddly shaped, which meant they needed revision (much like my poetry). I darted from inside the air-conditioned studio to the bright, sweltering sunshine of the New Mexico desert. Wielding a brick, I carefully broke shards into smaller pieces, arranging and rearranging until the halo felt complete. As I stepped back, tinges of blood trickling down my fingers, I knew this was it. This was what I had envisioned all along.

Day 5. Serendipitously, what I'd needed to complete the work had appeared. I arrived at our last workshop confident that the final step was only to adhere the glass to the board. A final meeting with Holly presented another challenge: if I planned to adorn the woman's head with glass AND create a permanent piece, I had no choice but to prepare a larger board. One problem- no larger boards were available. The only option was to make a trip to Lowe's, have another board custom cut, repaint, adhere the glass and wire to a new surface—all by 3:00.

After a trip to the big box store, I faced trying to recreate the original background color. Taking a deep breath, I offered up the piece to the creative gods and grabbed my paintbrush. That afternoon I was immersed in a process, a goal, a vision that previously existed only in my imagination. The background— the very same blue—the wire firmly attached, the body spun in age old yarn, all adorned with a halo. And around the face of my Aunt Josie, shattered glass made holy.

Homespun Mercies.

COLLAGE DESCRIPTIONS

What Do I Know of Love • page 10-11

One of the challenges of collage is communicating your intentions. I am much more comfortable letting the viewer wander through the images to surmise their own meaning, especially pieces that challenge me emotionally. This collage came on the heels of writing the poem. How do familial and societal views of gender, sex, and self shape our views of how and with whom we seek to find happiness and relationships during our lifetime? What happens when those constructs fall apart? This piece explores the idealized and sexualized relationships between men and women. While the collage has a darker undercurrent, it remains optimistic that love—in whatever form it takes—will ultimately win out.

Late at Night My Mind Goes Walking • page 34-35

It had been one of the most challenging seasons of my life. Seven years into marriage with my high school sweetheart, we decided to sell the 'family home' and start fresh. It was February of 2016, the spring of my junior year. In the midst of a 20-credit semester with a pending wedding, graduation, and study abroad trip to Ireland, adding house showings and daily cleanings stretched us thin. The realtor had assured us the house would take a while to sell. As luck would have it, we were flooded with showings and the house sold within thirty days. Thus began a whirlwind of packing, purging, and praying we would make it through. When we drove out of the driveway for the last time, we thought surely the worst was behind us. With all but the essentials in storage, we moved to an apartment nearby and a second one three weeks later. At night I would toss and turn, while my subconscious worked to make sense of it all. "Late at Night My Mind Goes Walking" was created after a cross-country move almost a year to the day, and soon became a metaphor for keeping the faith during times of transition.

Bacon Man • page 45

This collage came as a complete surprise. In the midst of a one-week course with collage artist Holly Roberts, I had been thinking—like many Americans—about the state of our country and the contentious nature of our politics. In the stack of magazine clippings I had brought along, there was an image of a proud Native American chief: headdress, piercing eyes, and a square jaw set. Stunning. What happened next I can't fully explain except to say that I began to deconstruct the image. I added the hair and hat of a 1940s farm girl, along with blue eyes looking askance, gold lips, and undersized sneakers, features that make folks laugh when they see it. But the hands—cut out from a page of an old dictionary—contain the real meaning: I was making the Indian chief look more like me while encapsulating the emasculation of an entire culture.

Lucretia • page 53

On our first date, my husband took me to the Minneapolis Institute of Arts to see one of his favorite paintings. The story is a sad one; Lucretia, the wife of a Roman nobleman, is raped by Sextus Tarquinius, son of the ruling tyrant. After summoning witnesses to disclose the act, Lucretia takes her own life, choosing death over dishonor. Rembrandt painted two images: one as she contemplates suicide; the next, immediately after she ends her life. The look of anguish on her face and the tears welled up in her eyes makes the pain palpable in Rembrandt's masterpiece, but, more importantly, in the hearts and souls of all victims of sexual violence.

Leaving Oz • page 71

"Leaving Oz" is one of my favorite pieces created at Anderson Ranch. I love how the background turned out—first painted a sunny yellow, followed by a mixture of mud and blue paint haphazardly spread across the canvas. To adequately portray both happiness and melancholy, I struggled to find images that would reflect opposite sides of this emotional spectrum. The face of the girl with the red bow perfectly captures what had personally plagued me for months. As the girl rises to new places and opportunities, those left behind can only watch from a distance.

Rock-a-bye Baby • page 76-77

If you grew up in the 1950s or 60s, the name Mother Goose is familiar and synonymous with nursery rhymes. In my childhood home, we sang the songs, read the books, and associated both with gender roles of the time. After our move to Colorado, I was thrilled to come across my collection of piano music, including a 1950s songbook of Mother Goose Nursery Rhymes. Even after so many years, the pastel images were familiar to me—anything but the first refrain, not so much. As I assembled this collage, I found myself playing with the phrases and was surprised by the outcome. Even the scrambled letters of Mother Goose took on new meaning.

An Apology to My Inner Poet • page 87

Procrastination is an issue for many writers and artists. My goal when writing this poem was to personify my muse as he becomes increasingly disgruntled by my lack of discipline (the use of "he" in relation to my inner poet is a discussion for another time). I like the boldness of the background, the overarching "assistance" of the unseen inner poet, and the apathy of the writer—perfectly summing up the daily challenge of life as a creative.

DANI WERNER PHOTOGRAPHY

DJ Hill is a freelance writer, photographer, poet, and mixed media artist. Her work has appeared in *Maple Grove, Route 66, Southwest Metro, St. Croix Valley, St. Louis Park,* and *White Bear Lake Magazines; The Atrium, Daily Sentinel, Red Bird Chapbooks Weekly Read, Red Flag Poetry,* and *The Rumpus;* and the anthologies *A View from Here: Poetry to Help You Soar, Worcestershire Poet Laureate Remembrance Anthology,* and JOMP21's *Dear Mr. President.*

DJ's collage and mixed media art have been included in exhibits at the R2 Gallery, Red Brick Center for the Arts, and other venues. Her poem "Harry" appears in the first edition of *Gone Dogs.* DJ lives and creates in Carbondale, Colorado. *Homespun Mercies* is her first collection of poetry.